WHY DO ANIMALS DO THAT?

101 Random, Interesting, and Wacky Things Animals Do -
The Facts, Science, & Trivia of Why Animals Do What
They Do!

SCOTT MATTHEWS

The more that you read, the more things you will know. The more you learn, the more places you'll go. - Dr. Seuss

Contents

Introduction

Have you ever marveled at the quirky and often perplexing behaviors of the animal kingdom? From the soothing purr of a cat to the mysterious wet noses of dogs, the world of animals is filled with captivating enigmas waiting to be unraveled. In *Why Do Animals Do That?* we embark on a delightful exploration into the curious and charming idiosyncrasies of the creatures we share our planet with.

This book invites you to join me on a journey of discovery, where we'll delve into the intriguing questions that have puzzled generations. We'll uncover the hidden purposes behind these behaviors and traits, shedding light on the secrets of evolution, adaptation, and survival.

So, let's embark on this adventure together, as we unveil the mysteries of the animal kingdom, one captivating revelation at a time. This book is an exploration of the remarkable, the extraordinary, and the heartwarming aspects of the natural world, where every page promises to leave you with a newfound appreciation for the enchanting creatures that share our world.

1. Why do chameleons change color?

Chameleons can change color to communicate with other chameleons, regulate their body temperature, and camouflage themselves in their environment. They do this by controlling the pigments in their skin and adjusting the reflectivity of their skin. Chameleons have cells in their skin called chromatophores, which contain pigments such as melanin, carotenoids, and pteridines. By expanding or contracting these cells, chameleons can change the color and pattern of their skin. They can also change the reflectivity of their skin by controlling the orientation of tiny, reflective crystals called iridophores.

The specific colors and patterns a chameleon displays can vary depending on the species and the context in which they are displayed. For example, a chameleon may turn bright colors to communicate aggression or courtship, or it may turn more subdued colors to blend in with its surroundings and avoid predators.

They are found in Africa, Madagascar, Europe, and Asia. They are also known for their long, protruding eyes, which are independently mobile and allow them to scan their surroundings in all directions. Chameleons have long, sticky tongues to catch insects and other small prey; in some species, the tongue is longer than the body!

2. Do crocodiles actually cry?

Crocodiles do produce tears, but they do not shed tears in response to emotions such as sadness or pain. Tears in crocodiles serve a different purpose, namely to keep their eyes moist and to wash away salt. Crocodiles live in both saltwater and freshwater environments, and their eyes can be exposed to saltwater while diving or feeding. Tears facilitate the removal of salt from their eyes, thereby preventing eye damage and maintaining clear vision. When crocodiles produce tears, they do not run down their faces like human tears, but instead collect at the corners of their eyes.

3. Why do ostriches dance?

Ostriches are large birds that are sometimes farmed for their meat. Recently, many videos have surfaced of ostriches doing a sort of "dance." When they do this, they lean backward and move from side to side. Their wings go up and down as they bob their heads. While their dances look very funny, they are very important in the lifecycle of the ostrich. Only male ostriches engage in dancing. This behavior serves as a kind of courtship display, with male ostriches dancing to attract female ostriches and express their interest. However, this doesn't quite explain why ostriches are also seen dancing when only people are around. When a male ostrich is kept away from female ostriches for a long time, they may sometimes show interest in animals that are not ostriches. This is because ostriches are often unable to tell whether or not certain creatures, such as humans, are from a separate species. Consequently, many people who have pet ostriches and farmers with a single ostrich on their farm find themselves occasionally greeted by a dancing ostrich.

4. Why do pigs roll in the mud?

Pigs love mud, but what precisely is the reason for their fondness? It's not just that they like it; they actually need mud to lead healthy, content lives, and there are several reasons for this. First, mud helps pigs regulate their body temperature. Pigs frequently spend extended periods in the heat and mud serves as a natural sunscreen, protecting their skin from sunburn. Also, the moisture in mud helps keep pigs cool via evaporative cooling, similar to how sweating works for humans. Second, wallowing in the mud helps get rid of parasites that are often found on pigskin. The mud acts as a sort of wash that removes the bugs. In addition, the mud helps to spread the smell of hormones that pigs produce. This is important when attempting to find a mate and claim territory. Finally, wallowing in mud is a social activity for pigs. They instinctively engage in this to bond with other pigs; without mud, this bonding is not as effective. Hence, mud is a necessary ingredient for having happy pigs.

5. Why do dogs play fetch?

There are a variety of reasons why dogs enjoy playing fetch, and there are a large number of reasons why some dogs may like it more than others. In general, it acts as exercise for the dogs. This releases feel-good chemicals in the dogs brain, similar to what humans feel when they have a good workout. In addition, the aspect of finding the ball and bringing it back activates the reward system in the dog's brain, making it feel accomplished. Scientists believe this mimics the feeling of bringing home fresh kills, which is something that wolves (ancestors of dogs) used to do frequently. Some breeds of dogs, such as retrieving and hunting dogs, have even more reason to enjoy the game. Retrieving dogs were bred to retrieve game animals that were hunted by their owner. Finding a toy during fetch replicates this retrieving behavior. In addition, fetch provides a bonding opportunity between a dog and one of their favorite humans. Most dogs enjoy this time to play and spend time with their favorite people.

6. Why do mockingbirds mock noises?

Perhaps you've heard mockingbirds mimic a variety of noises ranging from the sounds of other birds to the sounds of cars in the street or alarms going off in the distance. Some people question why these birds develop such an odd skill. Believe it or not, mockingbirds mimic all of these interesting sounds primarily for the purpose of mating. Male mockingbirds attract females via impressive feats of mimicry. Female birds appear to be more attracted to male birds if they can mimic a variety of sounds. Despite this, mockingbirds also have sounds that are unique to their species, with specific songs only sung by them. These unique songs serve the purpose of attracting mates, in addition to the various mimicry attempts made by male birds. Scientists are still not entirely sure why these acts of mimicry seem to be so attractive to female birds. Ongoing studies aim to unravel the purpose behind this unusual method of attraction.

7. Why do raccoons wash their food?

Videos all over the Internet show raccoons dipping food in water before eating it. Many people find this intriguing. Why would raccoons wash their food? Does it really help their food become cleaner? In reality, when raccoons dip their food in water to "wash it," they are not actually washing it at all. Instead, they are simply trying to gather information about what they are eating. Scientists realized this when they placed raccoons in an area with no water source to wash items with. The raccoons still went through the motions of washing the food. Further study showed that raccoons have hands that are very sensitive to touch. They use this sense to gather information about items, including their food. Wetting the items beforehand makes them easier for raccoons to feel and helps give them a better idea of what they are holding. Thus, they are not washing their food, but priming it for inspection!

8. Why do guinea pigs "popcorn"?

Popcorning is a term used to describe an action that pet guinea pigs often do. It happens when a guinea pig jumps in the air suddenly and bucks its back legs. Sometimes, they will repeat the behavior many times in a row before stopping. Guinea pigs do this primarily to show excitement or happiness. While younger guinea pigs are more likely to popcorn than their older counterparts, this behavior can be observed in guinea pigs of all ages. Occasionally, excessive popcorning can be seen as a sign of stress in these animals. If the popcorning is paired with whining or other indicators that the guinea pig is uncomfortable, it could indicate an attempt at self-soothing. However, if a guinea pig seems overall happy and only popcorns during times of play, it's generally considered a good sign that the pet is happy.

9. Why do wolves have packs?

Wolves are pack animals, staying together in groups throughout their entire lives. This way of living has many benefits for the wild canines. First, it makes it easier to raise pups. Wolf pups are often rambunctious and need a lot of attention. Raising them in a pack ensures that they will have enough adults around to keep them safe and fed. Second, hunting is easier in packs. When packs of wolves hunt, they can surround and herd their prey as needed. This would not be possible if a single wolf was left to hunt alone. The sheer size of the pack increases the likelihood of a successful hunt and makes the process significantly easier. Third, wolves are better able to defend their territory if they have a large pack. Lone wolves lack the ability to defend their territory from other animals that may wish to take over the area.

10. Why do some dogs have floppy ears and some don't?

Have you ever noticed how some dogs have ears that point up, some have ears that drop down, and some have ears that really flop down? There's a reason why dogs have different ear shapes. Humans selectively bred dogs for various roles in society, resulting in specific ear shapes. Some breeds have ears that are less prone to being grabbed, either standing up naturally or with the option for cropping. These dogs often work alongside potentially dangerous animals or individuals who might try to grasp them. Meanwhile, some dogs were bred with long, floppy ears, typically as scent hounds. These breeds were specifically developed for tracking prey using their exceptional sense of smell, and their elongated ears serve a functional purpose. The extended ears aid in dusting the ground during scent tracking, which helps them pick up scents they might otherwise miss.

Did You Know?

- Dolphins use unique signature whistles to identify themselves, like a name.
- Cows communicate with each other through a complex system of moos.
- Bats can eat up to 1,000 mosquitoes in an hour.
- Prairie dogs have a sophisticated system of communication with different calls for different predators.
- Bees perform a "waggle dance" to communicate the location of food sources to their hive.
- Some fish change their gender during their lifetime.
- Female hyenas are typically larger and more dominant than males.

11. Why do spiders spin webs?

There are over 45,000 known species of spiders and they can be found on every continent except Antarctica. While most spiders are harmless to humans, a few species have venom that can be harmful. Spiders are skilled hunters and use various techniques to catch their prey, including building webs, stalking and ambushing, and venomous bites. Some spiders can swim and even dive underwater to catch prey. They can regenerate lost or damaged legs and regrow them over time. They have multiple eyes, but their vision is not very good, and they rely on their sense of touch and the vibrations in their web to locate prey. Spiders are essential members of many ecosystems and help control pest populations. In addition to these features, spiders are also known for their ability to spin webs made of silk, a robust and flexible material produced by the spider's body. When an insect becomes trapped in the web, the spider can sense the vibration and will quickly move to subdue and wrap up its prey. The web also provides the spider with a place to live and lay eggs.

12. Why do whales make sounds, breach, and beach themselves?

Whales are some of the most fascinating and intelligent animals on the planet. There are over eighty known species of them, ranging in size from the pygmy sperm whale, which can be as tiny as 8-10 feet in length (2.4-3 meters), to the massive blue whale, which can grow to over 100 feet in length (30.4 meters) and weigh as much as 200 tons (the equivalent to about twenty-five full elephants).

One of the most unusual behaviors of whales is their ability to communicate through vocalizations or sounds. These vocalizations can serve various purposes, including communication, navigation, and finding food. Some whale species, such as humpback whales, are known for their complex songs, which can be heard from over twenty miles away (thirty-two kilometers) and last for hours.

Whales are also known for their impressive acrobatic abilities, such as breaching, where they launch themselves out of the water and crash back down with a huge splash. This behavior is believed to serve several purposes, including communication, socialization, and possibly even ridding themselves of parasites.

Despite their massive size, whales play essential roles in the ocean ecosystem. They help to spread nutrients throughout the ocean by eating tiny organisms at the bottom of the food chain and then excreting the nutrients near the surface. This helps support the growth of phytoplankton, a vital source of food for many other marine species.

In some cases, whales may accidentally beach themselves due to poor navigation, illness, or disorientation caused by human activities such as military sonar.

13. Why do squirrels bury their nuts?

Squirrels bury their nuts as a way of storing food for the winter when food may be scarce. They are known for their ability to find and store food, and burying nuts is just one of the ways they do this. Squirrels are opportunistic feeders and will eat a wide variety of foods, including nuts, seeds, fruits, and insects. During the fall, when food is plentiful, they will collect nuts and store them in caches to be used later when food is scarce. Squirrels are able to remember the location of their caches using a combination of spatial memory and scent. They use their sense of smell to locate the nuts they have buried, and they are able to remember the location of their caches even months later. Burying nuts also has the added benefit of dispersing seeds, which helps to promote the growth of new trees and plants. When squirrels forget or fail to retrieve some of the nuts they have buried, those nuts may germinate and grow into new trees.

14. Why do animals hibernate?

Animals hibernate to conserve energy and survive when food is scarce, or the weather is harsh. Hibernation is a state of reduced body activity and metabolism, during which an animal's body temperature, heart rate, and breathing rate decrease significantly. During hibernation, an animal's body uses stored fat and other energy reserves to survive, rather than needing to find food regularly. This allows the animal to survive during periods of food scarcity or harsh weather conditions, such as cold winters or dry summers. Hibernation is a strategy that is used by a variety of animals, including bears, bats, rodents, and some species of reptiles and amphibians. Each species has its specific requirements for hibernation, such as the amount of fat needed to survive, the length of time spent in hibernation, and the specific environmental conditions that trigger hibernation.

15. Why do birds fly in a "V" formation?

Have you ever noticed a flock of birds flying in a "V" formation and wondered what's going on? This behavior allows birds to conserve energy and improve their aerodynamics while in flight. Many birds, such as geese, ducks, and pelicans, use a "V" formation when flying, but not all birds do. When flying in a "V" formation, the bird at the front, called the "lead bird," flies into the wind and creates an area of low pressure behind it. The other birds in the formation then fly in the low-pressure area created by the lead bird, which requires less energy to maintain flight. In addition to conserving energy, flying in a "V" formation also helps birds improve their aerodynamics by taking advantage of the lift generated by the lead bird. While "V" formation flight is common among many bird species, some seabirds and birds of prey, opt for solitary or loosely dispersed flying patterns instead.

16. Why do roosters crow?

Roosters crow for various reasons, including announcing their presence to other roosters, establishing territory, and signaling to hens that it is time to start the day. They may also crow at other times of the day to announce their presence to other roosters or to establish territory. In addition, roosters may crow in response to external stimuli, such as loud noises or changes in lighting; for example, they may crow in response to the sound of an alarm clock or the opening of a door. Although roosters are well known for their ability to crow, they are not the only animals capable of making this type of sound. Some other animals known to crow or produce similar sounds include caciques (a type of tropical bird with unique crowing calls), marmots (large rodents known for their distinctive alarm calls, which can resemble crowing), and certain monkeys (such as howler monkeys, known for their loud and crowing-sounding calls).

17. Why do birds migrate?

Birds migrate to take advantage of seasonal changes in food availability, breeding opportunities, and a more suitable habitat. During the fall, many bird species migrate to warmer climates to escape the cold winter weather and to take advantage of more abundant food sources. In the spring, these same birds migrate back to their breeding grounds to breed and raise their young. The specific timing and route of a bird's migration can depend on various factors, including the species of bird, the latitude and altitude of its breeding and wintering grounds, and the availability of food and suitable habitat. Migration is an important adaptive trait that allows birds to survive and reproduce in changing environmental conditions. It's a complex behavior that requires a great deal of planning and preparation. It can be risky for birds, as they must navigate long distances and often face various challenges, such as predators and harsh weather.

18. Why do bees engage in pollination?

Bees pollinate flowers and other plants in order to collect nectar and pollen as food for themselves and their young. As bees move from flower to flower, they transfer pollen from the male reproductive structures of one plant to the female reproductive systems of another plant, which can lead to fertilization and the production of seeds. Pollination is a necessary process that allows plants to reproduce and produce seeds, which are necessary for the continuation of the species. It's also essential for the production of many of the foods that humans and other animals rely on, including fruits, vegetables, and nuts. In addition to collecting food, bees also benefit plants by helping to disperse their pollen and fertilize their flowers. This mutualistic relationship between bees and plants is an integral part of many ecosystems and is essential for the health and survival of both bees and plants.

19. Why do cats purr?

Cats purr for several reasons: to express happiness, comfort themselves, or create a bond with humans and other cats. This purring sound comes from the vibrations in their vocal cords within the larynx, or voice box. A cat typically purrs during exhaling, and the muscles in the larynx modulate the vibrations to produce the familiar purring noise. A relaxed, safe, or content cat will often purr, especially while being petted or when caring for kittens. Purring can also be a way for cats to manage stress and feel calmer in new or tense situations. Additionally, it's a way for them to communicate affection and strengthen their connection with those they are close to, using purring as a signal for attention and care from their owners or cat companions.

20. Why do dogs have wet noses?

Dogs have wet noses for several reasons. First, the moisture on a dog's nose helps to keep the nostrils moist, which is vital for maintaining healthy respiratory function. The nostrils can become dry and irritated if they are not kept moist, which can make it difficult for a dog to breathe and can lead to other respiratory problems. Second, the moisture on a dog's nose helps to regulate its body temperature. Dogs don't sweat through their skin the same way humans do, so they rely on other methods to regulate their body temperatures, such as panting and evaporative cooling. The moisture on their noses helps dissipate heat and relax the body, which is especially important on hot days or during strenuous activity. Finally, the moisture on a dog's nose can help to enhance its sense of smell. The moist surface of the nose helps trap and dissolve odorous molecules, which the olfactory receptors can then detect in the nose. A dry nose may be less effective at detecting odors, so dogs with dry noses may have a poorer sense of smell.

Did You Know?

- Male penguins often propose to their mates with pebbles.
- Sloths can hold their breath for up to forty minutes underwater.
- Male seagulls gift food to females as part of courtship.
- Crocodiles can't stick their tongues out.
- Parrots can learn and use human words and phrases.
- Female ferrets can die if they don't mate when in heat.
- Owls can rotate their heads up to 270 degrees.
- Meerkats take turns standing guard to watch for predators.
- Male emperor penguins huddle together to incubate their eggs in the harsh Antarctic cold.

21. Is it true that bulls don't like the color red?

Contrary to popular belief, bulls are not actually angered or agitated by the color red. In fact, bulls are color-blind to red and other colors, as they only see in shades of black, white, and gray. The reason why bullfighters wave a red cape during bullfights is not because of the color, but because of the movement of the cape, which is what attracts the bull's attention and prompts them to charge. The myth that bulls are angered by the color red likely originated from the use of red flags and capes in bullfighting, which is a traditional spectacle in Spain and other parts of the world. However, in reality, bulls are more likely to be agitated by sudden movements or loud noises, rather than by the color of an object.

22. Can a puffer fish kill you if you eat it?

Yes, it is true that certain species of puffer fish contain a potent toxin called tetrodotoxin, which can be deadly if ingested in sufficient quantities. Tetrodotoxin is a potent neurotoxin that can cause paralysis and respiratory failure, leading to death within a few hours in severe cases. Puffer fish are considered a delicacy in some cultures, such as Japan, where it is known as "fugu." However, preparing and serving it requires special training and certification due to the risk of tetrodotoxin poisoning. Chefs must undergo years of training and pass a rigorous exam to obtain a license to prepare and serve fugu. However, it's important to note that not all species of puffer fish contain tetrodotoxin.

23. Why do dogs sniff each others behind?

Dogs have a highly developed sense of smell that they use to gather information about their environment and other animals. When dogs sniff each other's behinds, they are actually collecting information about the other dog's identity, health, and emotional state. Dogs have a gland located near their anus that produces a unique scent that is specific to each individual dog. When one dog sniffs another dog's behind, they are able to pick up on this scent and glean information about the other dog's identity, including details like their age, gender, and overall health. In addition to identifying other dogs, sniffing each other's behinds can serve as a means for dogs to acquire insights into each other's emotional states. Dogs can pick up on chemical signals in the scent that indicate whether the other dog is feeling anxious, fearful, or relaxed, which can help them communicate and interact with each other more effectively.

24. Why do wombats poop cubes?

Wombats are unique among mammals in that they produce cube-shaped feces. This is due to the their specialized digestive system and the nature of their diet. Wombats are herbivores and feed mainly on tough, fibrous grasses, roots, and bark. To help break down these tough materials, their digestive system features a long and complicated intestine with multiple compartments. As food moves through these compartments, it's gradually broken down and compacted into small, dry pellets. The unique shape of wombat feces is due to the final stage of digestion, which takes place in the last section of the intestine. This section is more rigid than other parts, and as the feces are formed, they are compressed and molded into cube shapes. This allows the wombats to squeeze out as much moisture as possible from their feces, which is important in the arid regions of Australia where they live. The cube shape of wombat feces also have other benefits, such as allowing the feces to stack neatly and not roll away, which can help mark their territory and communicate with other wombats.

25. Why do oysters make pearls?

Oysters produce pearls as a defense mechanism against irritants such as parasites, sand, or other foreign objects that may enter their shells. When an irritant becomes trapped between the oyster's shell and its mantle, the oyster responds by secreting layers of a substance called nacre, also known as mother-of-pearl, around the irritant to protect itself. Over time, as the layers of nacre continue to accumulate, they form a pearl. The process of pearl formation can take several years, and the size and shape of the pearl will depend on the size and shape of the original irritant, as well as other factors such as the oyster's genetics and environment. While pearls are most commonly associated with oysters, other mollusks such as mussels and clams can also produce pearls in response to irritants. However, pearls from these other sources are less commonly used in jewelry.

26. Why do crabs walk sideways?

Crabs walk sideways as a result of their unique body structure and the way their legs are attached to their body. The legs of a crab are attached to the side of their body, rather than underneath like most other animals, which allows them to move sideways with ease. When a crab walks, it moves its front legs to the side, then pulls its body forward, and then repeats the motion with its back legs. This sideways movement is an efficient way for crabs to move across the ocean floor or over other surfaces, as it allows them to easily maneuver around obstacles and predators. In addition to their sideways walking, crabs are also able to move quickly in any direction by using their powerful hind legs to propel themselves forward or backward.

27. Can cows walk backward?

While cows are physically capable of walking backward, they do not do so frequently and may find it difficult or uncomfortable to do so. This is due to a combination of factors related to their physiology and behavior. One reason why cows may avoid walking backward is because they have large, heavy bodies with relatively small heads and short necks. This makes it more difficult for them to see where they are going when walking backward, and can make it harder to balance and coordinate their movements. In addition to their physical limitations, cows are also herd animals that rely on visual cues and social interactions with other cows to navigate their environment. Walking backwards may disrupt these social cues and make it harder for them to maintain their position in the herd or communicate with other cows.

28. Why do dogs rub their butts on the carpet?

Most dog owners have had moments where they turn around to see their precious pup rubbing their backside along the floor or carpet. While it can look funny, this action often has an important purpose. Dogs rub their backside along the floor in order to relieve irritation or pain in their behinds. This irritation can be due to a variety of reasons, but the most common is having impacted anal glands. These glands are a sort of identification tag for dogs, giving each a unique smell that other dogs can recognize. In addition, dogs can also express a small amount of fluid from these glands to mark their territory and claim items. Usually, the glands relieve themselves when the dog uses the restroom. However, some dogs have issues with this process and the glands become filled with fluid. When this happens, a dog will rub their bottom against the ground attempting to get relief. One way to stop this behavior is to have a veterinarian or groomer release the build-up of fluid in the glands.

29. Why do geckos lick their eyes?

Television shows portray geckos as wide-eyed lizards that obsessively lick their own eyeballs. Perhaps you have even witnessed geckos licking their eyes first hand in real life. Many people find this behavior to be funny, but geckos have an excellent reason for doing this. Geckos do not have eyelids. Like humans, however, geckos need to keep their eyeballs moist in order to have clear vision. These reptiles hunt mainly via using their sense of sight, making good vision important. In addition, they must use their sense of sight to stay safe from predators, as many larger animals eat geckos. They must lick their eyes to keep them moist, as well as to remove debris and cleanse them of irritants. Thus, in order to combat the dryness that is caused by not having eyelids and to prevent vision issues, geckos must lick their eyes regularly.

30. Why do cats use a litter box?

Since cats became common household pets, many non-cat owners have been grossed out at the thought of having a litter box in their house. Many ask why cats can't simply go to the bathroom outside like most dogs do. While some cats do prefer to go outside to relieve themselves, most will only go to the bathroom in a litter box. This is because, unlike dogs, cats have an instinct to bury their waste in order to hide their scent from predators. Historically, wildcats often had access to either sand or dirt. This allowed them to use the bathroom outside and then cover their waste in order to hide their tracks. Once domesticated, the environment changed. Outside cats no longer had access to loose dirt or sand. Inside cats, on the other hand, cannot cover their waste effectively if forced to use the bathroom on newspaper. This leads to cats using the bathroom on items that allow them to cover their waste after, such as clothing or blankets. Providing a litter box gives them a more enticing place to use the bathroom that allows them to cover their waste afterwards.

Did You Know?

- The Aye-Aye, a lemur species, has an elongated, bony middle finger used for tapping on trees to find insects.
- The geoduck, a type of clam, has one of the longest lifespans of any animal, up to 100 years.
- The narwhal's long tusk is actually a tooth that can grow up to ten feet (three meters) long.
- The mimic octopus can imitate the appearance and movements of other marine creatures.
- The blue-footed booby gets its name from its bright blue feet, which are used in courtship displays.

31. Why do hermit crabs change their shells?

Many hermit crab owners have the experience of buying a hermit crab in one shell, only to see it quickly switch to another shell in its tank after arriving home. There is a very good reason why this occurs. Hermit crabs continue to grow over time; however, the shells they inhabit are not living and do not grow with them. Pet stores often create tanks for their crabs that are meant to be temporary. They rarely include extra shells, meaning that if a crab grows while there, they may be stuck in a shell that is too small for them. In the wild, hermit crabs change shells regularly. They can often be seen trying multiple shells on before finally picking one to live in. This is why it is important to keep a variety of empty shells in your crabs tank should you ever own a hermit crab.

32. Why do fish float upside-down when they die?

Most fish owners will suddenly notice when a member of their tank has passed away and is now floating upside down at the top of the tank. The reason for this lies in fish anatomy and the process of decomposition. Fish are primarily made up of soft materials. When they decompose, the soft materials produce a lot of gasses, leading them to float in water. In addition, a lot of fish are naturally top-heavy. The only thing that keeps them correctly aligned while alive is their swim bladder. This is an organ on the bottom of their body that regulates how they float. When alive, this gives fish the ability to control how buoyant they are in water. Once they die, this organ stops functioning correctly. Occasionally, this organ malfunctions while the fish is still alive, leading to live fish floating and swimming upside down. If this happens, some diet changes, environment changes, and antibiotics can help restore your fish to normal functioning.

33. Why do cats meow?

Some people assume that cats meow in order to communicate with one another. In reality, this is not the case. Cats do not communicate with each other by meowing; instead, they communicate through a combination of nonverbal cues and some verbal communication, such as hissing and growling. Meowing, however, is only done in two instances. The first is when kittens are trying to communicate with the mother cat that something is wrong such as them being cold or frightened. Other than that, cats only meow at humans. Some scientists believe that this behavior stems from cats' attempts to emulate the sounds of human children, a phenomenon they attribute to the effects of domestication. Ancient cats saw how humans responded to their babies when they cried and learned to meow in order to elicit a similar response. Over time, this practice became encoded into cat behavior.

34. Why do hamsters burrow in bedding?

Most hamster owners will have moments when they suddenly can't find their little furry friend inside of the tank or cage. Oftentimes, they later locate their little friend hiding underneath objects or burrowed in their bedding. This is because wild hamsters are natural burrowers. Hamsters in the wild create large burrows and tunnels in order to keep themselves safe and provide an environment for sleep and storage. They have a weak sense of sight, which means that to stay safe from predators, they have to keep themselves hidden since they can't rely on their vision for assistance. In addition, burrows create the necessary level of warmth that keeps them comfortable. Studies have also shown that hamsters find the activity to be fun and will do it even when completely unnecessary. Some hamsters feel the need to borrow more than others. You may notice your furry friend constantly tunneling or only doing so to store food. Either way, it is important to provide plenty of bedding to a hamster so it has an opportunity to burrow if it desires to do so.

35. Why are moths attracted to light?

Moths are famously drawn to lights, a behavior known as phototaxis. This puzzling attraction is thought to be due to moths' evolutionary use of natural light, like the moon, for navigation. By flying at a constant angle to a celestial light source, moths can travel in straight lines. However, artificial lights disrupt this system; since they're much closer than the moon, they cause moths to circle endlessly around them. Some scientists also believe that the ultraviolet light from artificial sources mimics the UV patterns of flowers, which moths associate with food. This case of mistaken identity leads them toward light bulbs instead. The study of this phenomenon is crucial, as it can inform conservation efforts to minimize the negative impacts of artificial lighting on moth populations.

36. Why do dogs walk in circles before lying down?

Dogs may walk in circles before lying down to create a comfortable and secure sleeping area. By walking in circles, they can flatten grass or other vegetation and create a smooth surface on which to lie down. This may help them to feel more secure and comfortable while they are sleeping, especially if they are outside or in a new environment. Another reason for doing this is to align their body with the direction of the Earth's magnetic field. Some research has suggested that dogs and other animals may have a sense of the Earth's magnetic field and may use it to orient themselves in their environment. By walking in circles, dogs may be able to align their body with the direction of the magnetic field, which may help them to feel more secure and comfortable while they are sleeping. Finally, dogs may circle before lying down as a way to establish a sense of routine and familiarity. This behavior can in-still predictability and comfort, contributing to their overall sense of security.

37. Why do chinchillas need dust baths?

Some pets require more grooming than others and some have odd hygiene routines. One of the most unusual of these hygiene routines is known as a dust bath. Chinchillas are pets that cannot take regular baths because their fur holds so much moisture. In fact, this excess moisture is what leads chinchillas to require dust baths. Dust baths help remove some of the excess oil and moisture from the coats of chinchillas. Without taking these baths, their coats would become too moist, which could lead to fungal infections and other illnesses. This is also why pet chinchillas should not be allowed to get wet, as it will cause the dust baths to be less effective and lead to illness. Despite this odd manner of bathing, chinchillas are relatively clean pets. The dust baths aid in the removal of dirt and other substances in addition to simply eliminating moisture.

38. Why do snakes stick their tongues out?

Some people find snakes to be creepy, especially when these reptiles begin sticking their tongues out. It's common to see snakes slithering along, their tongues darting in and out of their mouths. However, there is a good reason for this behavior. Snakes have poor eyesight and a limited sense of hearing. To compensate for this, they rely on a special sense similar to the senses of smell and taste. Snakes possess a unique organ in the roof of their mouths called Jacobson's Organ, which processes various chemicals and compounds in the air to provide the snake with information about its environment. Snakes flick their tongues to collect tiny particles from the air, which stick to their moist tongues when they come into contact with saliva. They then use their tongue to bring the particles to the Jacobson's Organ, where they can process the information and learn more about what's happening around them.

39. Why do cats hiss?

It's said that cats hiss to express that they aren't happy. They make this noise by releasing a short spurt of air through their mouths while baring their teeth and flattening their ears. There are several reasons why cats might hiss. Usually, it's the first attempt to warn somebody or something that they don't like something that is going on. This is a way that a cat expresses that they might attack if the unpleasant action continues. However, this is not always the case. Sometimes cats hiss because they have no other way to express what they are feeling. This sometimes happens when they are in pain or are stressed out. This could be a warning that they will attack, or it could simply be them communicating their discomfort. Cats sometimes hiss at each other to express that they don't like something another cat is doing. During some instances, like rough play, this can be a simple indicator to the other cat that they should calm down a bit.

40. Why do fish sleep with their eyes open?

One of the biggest shocks that young fish owners get when they see their fish sleeping for the first time is that their fish's eyes are wide open. The truth is, fish do not sleep with their eyes open. They don't actually have eyelids at all. Unlike humans and other land-bound animals, fish don't really have a need for eyelids. They are in water which helps regulate the level of moisture their eyes need, and they also need less protection from the sun. There are a few fish species that have eyelids, such as sharks, but these are in the minority. In addition, fish don't technically sleep in the way that people do. Instead, certain parts of their brain go into a period of rest. Some fish enter periods of stillness or lethargy when this happens. Other fish, however, will keep moving during these rest periods as their ability to filter oxygen from the water relies on their movement.

Did You Know?

- Male seahorses give birth to their young.
- Male anglerfish fuse with females, becoming parasites that provide sperm.
- The Surinam toad carries its eggs on its back in pockets of skin.
- Male emperor penguins incubate eggs on their feet, fasting for two months.
- Female sea turtles return to the same beach where they were born to lay their eggs.
- Male clownfish change sex to become females when the dominant female dies.

41. Why do only male lions grow a mane?

Lions are large predatory cats that are found primarily in the open plains of Africa, and often also in zoos around the world. These creatures are known to be ferocious and majestic, with one of the defining features of the species being the glorious mane that grows from the necks of adult male lions. However, many individuals wonder why only male lions grow manes. Male lions grow manes due to the production of testerone, a hormone in the body that female lions naturally lack. Occasionally, female lions will have a hormonal imbalance and will also grow a mane due to having excess testosterone, although this is rare. Male lions benefit from having manes as it allows them to seem larger as they age, which can help scare off competition. The manes also serve as protection during male lion conflicts for dominance, preventing them from causing serious harm to each other.

42. Why do electric eels make electricity?

Eels are a type of oddly shaped fish that are found in the ocean. With bodies somewhat similar to snakes, they are often long and have fearsome teeth and jaws. However, some eels also have a special trait that can seem unbelievable at times. Electric eels are a type of eel that can naturally produce electricity in their bodies and use it to shock other creatures. This is attributed to the presence of special cells in the eels' bodies called electrocytes, which are controlled by their nervous system. When the eel senses prey or a threat, it sends a signal to the cells to activate. Each cell only produces a small amount of electricity, but when paired together, the effect builds. This enables eels to deliver powerful shocks to both prey and predators. They can generate up to 600 volts of electricity, enough to kill a human! Don't fear, however. There have been very few reported cases of electric eels attacking humans.

43. Why do jellyfish sting?

Jellyfish are unique sea creatures that move along with the currents, unable to make drastic movements on their own. However, while these creatures may appear docile, they are actually capable of inflicting great pain on humans and animals that come into contact with them. Jellyfish are capable of stinging, and they do so by using microscopic spikes inside of their tentacles called nematocysts. When they feel movement, the spikes deploy and release venom into whatever touches the jellyfish. Some jellyfish produce mild venom that only causes minor pain and itching. Others produce venom that can be deadly to full-grown humans. However, jellyfish do not sting people to cause harm; instead, they employ this ability for hunting. Their stings paralyze small prey, enabling them to capture it despite the jellyfish's slow movement. Additionally, the stings serve as a defense against predators that might attempt to prey on the jellyfish. All of the stings that happen to humans are simply unfortunate accidents.

44. Why do bees make honey?

Honey is a delicious treat in the human world as well as in the bee world. The sugary, sweet liquid is often used in breakfast items, desserts, and special sauces around the world. While humans love honey for its flavor, bees love it for a different reason. Honey is created when bees eat nectar and digest it in a special organ called "the honey stomach." This breaks down the nectar into the sugary substance known as honey. The bees then regurgitate the honey and pass it from bee to bee until it is eventually deposited into a honeycomb. Honey is created to act as a food source when nectar is not available, such as during cold winter months. Without turning nectar into honey first, it would go bad before it could be used for food. Thus, bees create honey to ensure that they will have a source of food that is long-lasting and provides the nutrients they need to survive.

45. Why do whales sing?

Whale songs are known in the human world as relaxing noise. However, they hold a much greater importance to the whales that sing them. Whales sing to communicate with one another. In water, the senses of sight, smell, and touch are limited. Thus, many sea creatures rely on sound as their primary sense. Whales are unique in their communication as they make their sounds in patterns that can be identified and recorded. Overall, the primary purpose of whale song is to entice other whales to mate. However, whales also sing to navigate their surroundings through echolocation and for general communication with each other. Mother whales will even sing to their offspring to soothe them. Recently, scientists have discovered that sometimes whales even sing for fun. However, why do humans like these whale songs so much? The whale songs tend to have similar compositions to many of our favorite human songs!

46. Why do stink bugs stink?

The brown marmorated stink bug is an insect that is capable of producing a disgusting odor. Many people fear that these insects are dangerous, but this is not the case. The stink bug has a special organ in its abdomen that produces chemicals when activated, creating a strong, foul-smelling odor. The stink bug then releases this odor if it feels threatened. Stink bugs cannot pinch, bite, or sting; their odor is their only defense against predators. Many animals try to eat stink bugs but are quickly repelled by their sudden odor release. Unfortunately for humans, simply scaring a stink bug can be enough to activate their defense system. Startled stink bugs will happily spray their odor anytime they feel cornered or threatened, leading to many stinky false alarms. Occasionally, the chemicals that cause the smell can cause skin irritation in humans, but overall the bug is harmless.

47. Why do caterpillars sting?

Many people fear caterpillars because of the stories they hear about their painful stings. However, not all caterpillars sting, and those that do have a good reason. Caterpillars are larvae that will eventually turn into butterflies or moths. When fully grown, these bugs can fly away from danger quickly. As larvae, however, they move very slowly. Thus, when predators attack caterpillars, they are unable to run away. Some species of caterpillars combat this by stinging. These caterpillars produce poison in special sacs that connect to sharp, hair-like organs on their body. When these hairs are stimulated, the poison is released, and the caterpillar stings. This often deters potential predators from attacking the caterpillar. It can even prompt predators that are in the process of eating the caterpillar to cease and spit them out, as the poison is injected into their mouths.

48. Why do seagulls show up far away from the beach?

Seagulls are most often found near the ocean. However, sometimes people will notice these beach-loving birds flying around in places that are nowhere near the sea at all. This can happen for a few reasons. First, seagulls sometimes fly inland to evade approaching storms. Storms can be dangerous and seagulls may sense this danger and flee to avoid it. Next, seagulls will sometimes fly to find better nesting places. If nesting spots or materials cannot be found near the shore, these birds may migrate further inland to find good spots or to locate needed materials. Third, seagulls will sometimes go inland to find food. Occasionally, hunting for food in the ocean may not result in success. Seagulls will search elsewhere if this happens in order to secure food if needed.

49. Why do crows like shiny things?

Crows will often collect shiny trinkets. This habit has baffled many bird watchers over the years. However, many scientists claim that this is not necessarily a normal behavior for a crow, but instead an indicator that the crow is young. Young crows are known to be curious and will often pick up objects that have no true value to them. They will then hide these objects or spend time pecking at them in order to explore them. Adult crows do not display this same level of curiosity and will not take shiny objects; instead, they will only pick up and hide food items. However, sometimes these items are wrapped in foil or similar materials, leading people to also believe that they are picking them up because they are shiny.

50. Why do coyotes come into the city?

Coyotes are a type of wild canine that are similar to wolves but are significantly smaller and more timid. However, they are still dangerous. Recently, coyotes have begun migrating into cities. While coyotes are generally afraid of humans, they are opportunistic hunters and have been attacking pets in urban areas. Many people wonder why these animals are suddenly becoming an issue. Scientists claim this is happening for two reasons: first, coyotes are attracted to our food; and, second, they have noticed a lack of predators in populated areas. Trash cans and dumpsters are great sources of food for these canines, leading them to leave the wilderness in order to benefit from human food waste. In addition, some humans have begun directly feeding coyotes, causing them to view humans as a direct source of food. Finally, coyotes are safer in urban areas as their natural predators cannot find them there. With an abundance of food and no need to fear being hunted, coyotes unfortunately have begun calling cities their new homes.

Did You Know?

- Female green anacondas are significantly larger than males.
- Flamingo chicks are initially born with gray feathers. They gradually turn pink as they grow due to their diet primarily consisting of crustaceans and algae rich in pigments.
- Male ferrets must mate with females to avoid health problems.
- Female whip-tail lizards can reproduce without males, through parthenogenesis.
- A newborn kangaroo is about the size of a lima bean and is born prematurely.
- Female bees lay eggs that become workers, while the queen bee lays eggs that become new queens.

51. Why do foxes scream?

Foxes are members of the canine family that act a bit differently from other canines. While most domestic dogs bark and most wild canines howl, foxes do neither; instead, they often scream. In fact, foxes scream in a manner so loud and human-like that their vocalizations have been known to startle humans who hear them, often leading people to mistake the sounds for those of a human. As frightening as it may be, foxes need to make these screams to communicate; they talk to one another with these noises, expressing a desire to mate or a fear of danger. Without making these noises, foxes would be unable to find breeding partners and would be unable to warn their fellow creatures of potential threats. They also use their screams to scare away predators when attempting to defend their territory, which can help them avoid dangerous, violent encounters.

52. Why do greyhounds race?

Greyhound racing was once an extremely popular sport. However, recently it has fallen out of favor and is often only done on an amateur level for fun. Greyhounds originally did not race but instead participated in a type of hunting called coursing. This is when dogs use their sense of sight to chase after prey. Eventually, hunting using sight hounds became less popular and instead people began to find other uses for the dog. With the invention of the mechanical rabbit, the sport of greyhound racing was born. The dogs are placed on an oval track, and a fake rabbit is pulled around the track in order to stimulate the dogs' prey drives. The dogs chase the rabbit, and the dog that crosses the finish line first is declared the winner. Dogs often race like this until they grow old, then they are retired and adopted by loving families.

53. Why do some monkeys hang from their tails?

There are many types of monkeys, each with different traits. Some, known as "new world monkeys," have the ability to hang from their tails thanks to a prehensile tail. Prehensile tails can grasp objects and function somewhat like a hand. Therefore, some monkeys use their prehensile tails to hang upside down, relying on their tails' gripping ability, similar to a hand. This process is aided by a special patch of bald skin that helps the monkeys maintain friction. Some new world monkeys lack this patch but are still able to hang from their tails. They cannot, however, use their tails to pick up objects like monkeys with bald patches can sometimes do.

54. Why do sloths move so slowly?

Sloths are known for their docile personalities and slow movements. Many people wonder how they manage to survive despite their slow speed and apparent laziness. In reality, sloths depend on their slowness to survive. They consume low-calorie food and have a slow metabolism. It can take a sloth the entire day to digest just one meal. This means that they cannot afford to burn large amounts of energy with excessive movement. Hence, their slow movements and the way they stay still in between helps them properly conserve energy. In addition, their slow movements appear to help them avoid making mistakes, as they have poor eyesight and cannot quickly process what they are seeing. By moving slowly, sloths stay safer and are able to avoid making mistakes such as walking into a predator's field of vision.

55. Why do camels have humps?

Most movies set in a desert landscape contain scenes that show camels walking in the distance. These camels always have either one hump or two sitting on their backs. Camels have humps for several reasons. The primary purpose is to store fat for future use, serving as energy reserves when food may be scarce. The fuller and healthier the camel, the more substantial its humps will be. In addition, the camels' humps also store water, which can sometimes become scarce in the desert environment. This water storage allows camels to go without water for longer periods without dehydration. Finally, camels' humps help them regulate their temperature; the fat insulates them and protects them against temperature extremes.

56. Why do giraffes have long necks?

Giraffes are known to have the longest necks in the animal kingdom. Scientists were initially baffled by the sheer length of the animal's necks but were eventually able to determine two reasons why giraffes need these long appendages. First, giraffes evolved to have longer necks to compete with other species. Specifically, herbivores (plant-eating animals) were having issues competing for food during the time when giraffes began to develop longer necks. There was not enough plant material within reach for everyone. Giraffes developed their long necks to reach higher plant material and ensure survival. In addition, scientists have recently discovered that their long necks play a role in handling conflict. Giraffes fight by slamming their long necks into each other which is how they compete with one another for mates.

57. Why do dogs beg for table food?

Dogs are known to be man's best friend, and like man, they love food. Pet owners often have to deal with excited pups begging at the table each night at dinner or nervously eyeballing their sandwiches during lunch, even if the food they want is not good for them. Why do dogs do this? Like humans, dogs enjoy the taste of certain foods, but also do not have the capability to understand that some types of food are bad for them. Thus, anything that smells delicious to a dog will entice them to beg. Some dogs may do this by trying to get closer to food to steal a bit, while others may whine or simply stare and drool. Dogs often beg in ways that owners unknowingly reward. For example, a dog that is given food for being cute may give "puppy dog eyes" to their owners if they want a bite of their hamburger. Hence, dogs beg because they enjoy human food and employ different begging techniques based on their past success in obtaining food.

58. Why do opossums pass out when afraid?

Opossums are marsupials that have a unique talent: passing out when afraid. Although many people assume that they are merely pretending to be asleep, this is not actually the case. Opossums do fall into a state where they cannot move or act when they are frightened. Their bodies go limp. They will sometimes release all the waste from their body in the form of urine or stool. They will breathe slowly and shallowly to make it seem like they are dead. They also often will leave their eyes wide open and stop blinking. This is referred to as a catatonic state. Opossums go into this state because they cannot defend themselves against predators. So, instead of trying to do so and potentially getting hurt, opossums' bodies try to convince other animals that they are dead and no longer good to eat. In addition, most predators are confused by the display, which gives the marsupial a chance to escape while the predator is distracted.

59. Why do octopuses have beaks?

While birds are known for having beaks, they are not the only animals to have them. In fact, some animals that live in the sea share this body part with their avian cousins. Octopuses are cephalopods that live in the ocean and have beaks. Many people are unaware that octopuses have beaks, as they keep them hidden underneath their bodies and are able to pull them back inside of their bodies when not in use. However, without beaks, octopuses could not even survive. Octopuses, being carnivores, consume other animals to sustain themselves and survive. Many of the animals that octopuses consume are encased in hard shells for protection. Therefore, having a beak helps octopuses break open these tough shells, allowing them to feed on a variety of creatures, from crabs to clams. After breaking open the shells of their food, octopuses then use their beak to break their food into smaller bites. Hence, their beak is their primary tool for opening and eating their food.

60. Why do squids make ink?

Movies love to show squids spurting out ink as they swim in the ocean. However, do squids really spray ink? The answer is yes. Squids have a special organ in their body called an ink gland. In this special organ, ink is made by combining melanin (for color) and mucus (for consistency). Meanwhile, they also have another special organ called an ink sack to hold the ink they make. This sack is connected to a special muscle called a sphincter which allows them to release the ink if needed. When squids feel threatened, they release a stream of this ink to distract whatever is threatening them. This gives them a chance to flee and escape the danger. Believe it or not, humans also benefit from squid ink. We use the dark pigment in many of our food items and beauty products; but don't worry, we remove the pigments before mixing them with mucus!

Did You Know?

- Dogs' sense of smell is 10,000 to 100,000 times more sensitive than humans'.
- Cats can rotate their ears 180 degrees.
- Some species of snakes can detect infrared radiation to "see" heat.
- Bats use echolocation to navigate and find prey.
- Elephants can communicate using low-frequency infrasound that travels long distances.
- Sharks can detect electrical fields produced by living organisms.
- Pigeons can recognize themselves in a mirror.

61. Why do starfish regrow limbs?

When most animals lose a limb, they are simply stuck without that limb for the rest of their lives. Starfish, however, have a special ability that allows them to regrow lost limbs. Recently, it has even been discovered that some starfish can regrow their entire nervous system if necessary. This means that some species can regrow their entire body if only a single limb is left. Starfish do this by first using special cells to clot the injured area and prevent fluid loss. Next, cells called myocytes from other body parts travel to the injured area. These cells move into place to act as new tissue to regrow the limb. Then, they change in order to fit the needs of the limb, becoming more like cells around them than the cells where they initially came from. This ability allows starfish to survive attacks and flee even if it costs them a limb.

62. Why do praying mantises eat the heads off their mates?

One of the most common facts that people know about praying mantises is that the females of the species will supposedly eat the head of their mate once the mating process is over. While this is true in some circumstances, it is not always the case. Praying mantises do not kill their mates in the wild. Instead, they will mate and then part ways without any violence. However, if a praying mantis couple is kept in captivity, the female may eat the male's head after they breed. This is due to the stress of being held captive as well as the competition for resources in a limited environment. In order to ensure the survival of herself and her potential babies, the female mantis will kill the male to avoid having to fight him for resources such as food and water. In addition, the male's head provides some extra nutrition to the female mantis, ensuring she remains healthy enough to produce offspring. Once the limitations of captivity are removed, however, this behavior is not observed in the species.

63. Why do termites swarm?

Termites are insects that often feed on wood. These insects tend to swarm during certain parts of the year and enter into people's houses. While it is a pain for humans to deal with, this behavior is important to the termites. Termites, like many insects, are always seeking out new food sources as old food sources grow scarce. They swarm in order to move to previously non-inhabited areas so that food competition is no longer an issue. They will move in large groups and colonize new areas, intending to stay and feed off of the food available there. Some termites, such as drywood termites, can pose a significant threat to human existence by targeting the very wood we use to construct our homes. Swarms of these termites can be highly destructive to homeowners, as termites are known for their capacity to cause extensive damage. It's worth noting, not all termite swarms are a cause for concern, as many of them do not feed on dry wood, making them more of an annoyance than a problem.

64. Why do grasshoppers become locusts?

While people often view grasshoppers as docile and harmless creatures, locusts are viewed as terrifying pests. Many people do not realize that grasshoppers and locusts are the same creatures, just in different forms. When food is scarce, grasshoppers cluster tightly to feed on what little is available, their bodies rubbing together, a contact that signals them to recognize the shortage of food. After this, their bodies begin to undergo changes. These changes prompt grasshoppers to band together and become nomadic, allowing them to fly in search of new food sources. However, because of the large number of locusts in a swarm, this often leads to entire fields of crops being eaten, creating additional hardships for other animals in the area. Therefore, humans do their best to prevent grasshoppers from forming locust swarms. However, locusts continue to act as pests during times of famine and are still feared in places all over the world.

65. Why do snakes shed their skin?

Have you ever found snake skin while walking around outside? Many people associate the active shedding of skin with snakes. All reptiles shed their skin, but unlike mammals that tend to shed their skin in flakes, they shed it in large pieces. Sometimes these pieces consist of the entirety of the skin on their body. This is because a reptile's skin does not grow with the rest of its body. In order for reptiles to be able to continue to grow, they must sometimes be able to shed their skin in a manner that is rapid and sudden, in a matter of hours to days, allowing them to continue growing in a way that is safe. Reptile shedding also has one additional bonus: it helps them prevent parasitic infections. By shedding their skin they also shed any parasites that may be attached to the skin.

66. Why do flamingos stand on one leg?

Even lawn flamingo decorations depict the pink bird standing on one leg, which is indeed an accurate portrayal of these birds. They often stand on one leg for a few reasons. One reason is because it helps prevent fatigue. By alternating legs, flamingos give one leg a chance to rest while the other leg holds the weight of the bird. In addition, standing on one leg helps distribute heat throughout the flamingo's body. The ground is often hot and the more parts of the flamingo's body that touches the ground, the hotter the flamingo will be. Standing on only one leg reduces the amount of a flamingo's body that touches the hot ground, allowing them to be cooler. Alternatively, when it is cold outside, holding one leg closer to the flamingo's body allows it to retain extra body heat.

67. Why do hens get broody?

Broody hens, intent on hatching and raising their own chicks, can become aggressive when humans attempt to collect their eggs. This behavior isn't solely linked to the presence of fertilized eggs; it can be triggered by various factors. For instance, the sight of baby chicks or eggs left in the nest for too long can induce broodiness. Even environmental conditions like light and temperature changes can prompt this maternal instinct. While broody hens are generally harmless, they pose a challenge for farmers trying to harvest eggs.

68. Why do parrots talk?

Parrots are well known for their ability to speak. However, can they really talk like humans can? Parrots cannot communicate with speech in the way that humans can. While they can make certain words and sounds, they are often unable to understand what they mean. Some parrots however, can understand and use words and sounds, but their vocabulary is very limited compared to that of a human. But how do parrots make sounds? Parrots do not have vocal cords like humans have; instead, they have a special organ called a syrinx. This gives them the ability to make far more sounds than even humans can make. When parrots were domesticated by humans, they started copying the sounds they were hearing from their owners. Thus, parrots raised in captivity can often say a few words and may even be able to understand what certain words mean. Wild parrots, on the other hand, mimic noises that are natural to the environment that they are in.

69. Why can't penguins fly?

Penguins are flightless birds that live in the southern hemisphere. When people hear the word "bird," they usually immediately think of flying. However, there are some species of birds out there who do not fly. Penguins are one such species, and that's because their wings are used for something far more important given the environment that they live in, which are environments commonly filled with water. While they primarily live on land, they spend a lot of their time hunting and traveling via the ocean. Therefore, when other birds developed the ability to fly, penguins developed wings that instead helped them swim. Their wings, paired with their water-resistant feathers, make penguins able to glide through the water effortlessly. This allows them to quickly escape predators and rapidly navigate the underwater world. Furthermore, due to the way penguins' weight is distributed, even if they had wings capable of flight, they would likely still be unable to take to the skies.

70. Why do peacocks have fancy tails?

Peacocks are known for their beautiful tails. They are the male birds of the peafowl species, a type of pheasant known for their large and colorful back feathers. Female peafowl, on the other hand, do not have bright feathers like male peacocks do. The reason that only male birds of the species have these fancy, colorful feathers is that they are used to attract females. When attempting to find a mate, male peacocks will spread their back feathers in a beautiful display of color and extravagance. The females are often attracted to the males with the most colorful feathers. Size also plays a role in the partner that the female bird will choose, as peacocks with larger feathers are more attractive to female peafowls. However, tails that are too colorful or too large can be intimidating to the females. As a result, males with decently colorful and modestly sized feathers tend to fair best when it comes to mating.

Did You Know?

- Koalas primarily eat eucalyptus leaves, which are toxic to most animals.
- The vampire bat feeds on the blood of other animals.
- A group of vultures feeding together is called a wake.
- The binturong, or "bearcat," smells like buttered popcorn.
- Some birds, like the secretary bird, are opportunistic carnivores and eat snakes.
- The hagfish can produce copious amounts of slime to deter predators.
- The hoatzin, a bird found in the Amazon, has a digestive system that ferments its food.

71. Why do some crawfish have a blue color?

Most crawfish depicted in the media and found in the grocery store are red. However, there are variations in color, including blue and white. These different colors appear whenever the cells that produce the pigment of the exoskeleton malfunction. A normal amount of pigment makes a crawfish red; a slightly smaller amount of pigment makes it blue; a significantly smaller amount makes the crawfish white. The way that the cells behave depends on the oxidation that they receive. If the cells do not receive enough oxygen, less pigment will be produced. Overall, blue crawfish are rare, appearing in only one out of 50,000 crawfish. White crawfish are even rarer and are estimated to only appear in one out of every five million crawfish.

72. Why do crabs have one claw that is bigger than the other?

Have you ever seen a crab with one big claw and one little claw? This is very common in male crabs, and is even more common in certain species such as fiddler crabs. There are a few reasons why it benefits these crabs to have one large claw and one smaller. The smaller claws are actually the normal size for the species, and female crabs often have claws of this smaller size. Male crabs will grow an extra large claw in order to attract mates, provide a method of defense against other crabs and predators, and provide a way to intimidate rival crabs. Male crabs will wave their large claw around when attempting to attract mates. Female crabs are often attracted to the male crabs with the largest claw. Moreover, male crabs often use their large claws to fight off predators as well as to fight each other when necessary. These large claws make excellent weapons. The claws are also useful for intimidation, as larger crabs use them against smaller ones.

73. Why do some cats have extra toes?

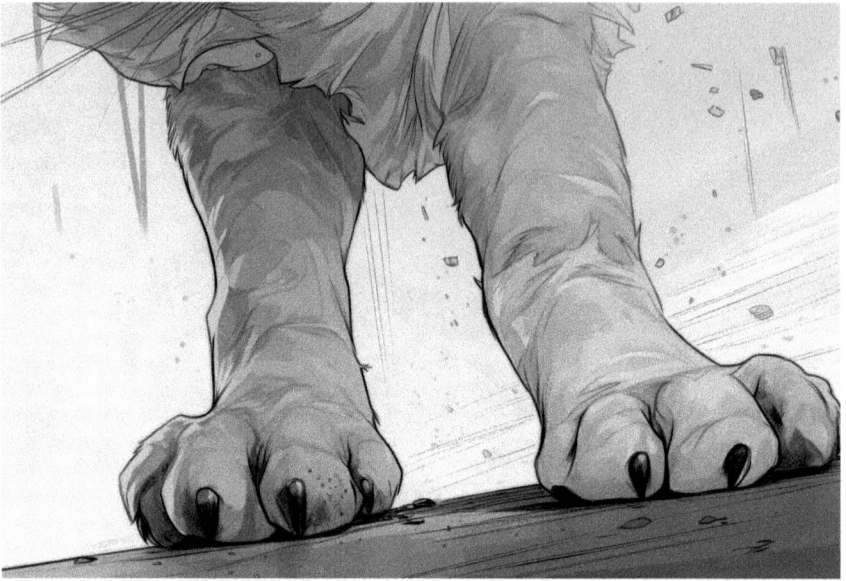

Although most cats typically have eighteen toes in total, some cats boast a few extra toes, earning them the title of "polydactyl cats." These felines are often appreciated for their distinctive characteristics, and some people actively seek them out as pets. Polydactyl cats are created whenever there is a dominant gene for the trait passed down through a bloodline. Thus, breeders can usually guess if a litter of kittens will contain any polydactyl kittens as polydactyl parents often pass the trait down. These cats are somewhat more common in port cities all over the world, as sailors often traveled with them, believing they brought good luck. Because of the way that the polydactyl gene is passed down, entire populations of stray cats in these areas often have the trait. Some pet owners become distressed when they realize that their feline friend has some extra toes, but ultimately, having a polydactyl cat rarely causes issues. The extra toes cause no pain and do not impair the quality of life of the cat.

74. Why do some dogs have smushed faces?

Many people choose to buy dogs like pugs or bulldogs because they are attracted to their flat, smushed faces. Others may wonder about the specific appeal of these breeds' facial features. Breeds such as pugs and bulldogs have smooshed faces because that is how we have selectively bred them. Certain dog breeds, like bulldogs, were intentionally bred to have flat faces for a particular reason. Bulldogs were specifically bred for bullfighting, and their flat faces served a functional purpose in this context. Having flat faces with no protrusions made it more challenging for the bulls to grip and toss the bulldogs during fights, ultimately helping to keep the dogs safe. Other breeds, such as pugs, were bred to have flat faces for the purposes of looking aesthetically pleasing or cute. Many of these flat-faced breeds today have been bred into having even flatter faces than they were initially supposed to have. This has led to an increase in breathing problems in dogs of these breeds.

75. Why do some ladybugs bite?

Have you ever had a ladybug land on you and then suddenly felt a sharp bite? The reason this "ladybug" bit you is that it's not actually a ladybug. There are multiple species of insects that look like ladybugs but are not ladybugs at all. One of the species, the Asian lady beetle, is known to bite more often than others. You can tell the difference between these bugs and actual ladybugs by their color. Ladybugs are red with black spots, while Asian lady beetles instead have an orange or yellow color. Asian lady beetles are often slightly oval-shaped and larger than ladybugs as well. Ladybugs also have a primarily black head, while Asian lady beetles, on the other hand, have a white head with a black "M" on it. By being able to identify Asian lady beetles, you can prevent yourself from being bitten by them and continue to enjoy the presence of actual ladybugs without the risk of a bite.

76. Why do hummingbirds have long beaks?

Hummingbirds are small birds with extremely long beaks. Many people get excited to see them fluttering around drinking nectar from various plants in the area. The reason that hummingbirds have these long beaks is related to their need to gather nectar, and they do so with a long tube-like tongue. Their beaks exist to hold their tongues and aid them in digging into flowers. Specifically, they tend to enjoy drinking nectar from flowers that are shaped as a sort of trumpet or cone. If their beaks were shorter, they would be unable to reach the nectar in the type of flowers that they tend to drink from. Some hummingbirds have shorter beaks than others. Scientists have found that these birds seek out in particular flowers that match the approximate length of their beaks. Birds with shorter beaks will seek out smaller flowers and birds with larger beaks will avoid smaller flowers in search of larger ones.

77. Why do isopods roll into a ball?

Isopods (also known as pill bugs and rollie-pollies) are small invertebrates that roll into a ball when handled. Many children grow up playing with these bugs and find them to be rather cute little creatures. However, these bugs do not enjoy being played with. Isopods tend to roll into a ball whenever they feel threatened. This is because their underbellies are significantly softer and more sensitive than the hard shell on their back. By rolling into a ball, they protect their underbelly and only expose their hard shell to the predators, making them significantly harder to eat. Additionally, curling into a ball like shape can help the bug retain moisture. This is incredibly important for land-dwelling isopods as they are not surrounded by water like their sea-dwelling cousins are. If for some reason the isopods are unable to roll into a ball, they risk potentially drying out and dying.

78. Why do some fish live in saltwater and some live in freshwater?

Have you ever wondered why some fish only live in freshwater and some only live in saltwater? Over the years, fish have evolved to adapt to their environment. Thus, saltwater fish have significantly more salt in their bodies than freshwater fish. However, many people wonder why freshwater fish and saltwater fish cannot live in the same environment as each other. The answer lies in a process referred to as osmosis. Essentially, if there is a group of cells that has more salt in them near a group that has less, the water from the less salty group will travel into the salty cells in an attempt to balance the ratio of salt to water. So if a saltwater fish was placed in freshwater, their cells would absorb too much water when trying to find balance. In a similar manner, if a freshwater fish was placed in salt water, all of the water in their cells would flow out to try to find balance with the salt water outside of them. Both instances would lead to the death of the fish.

79. Why do dogs have an extra claw behind their legs?

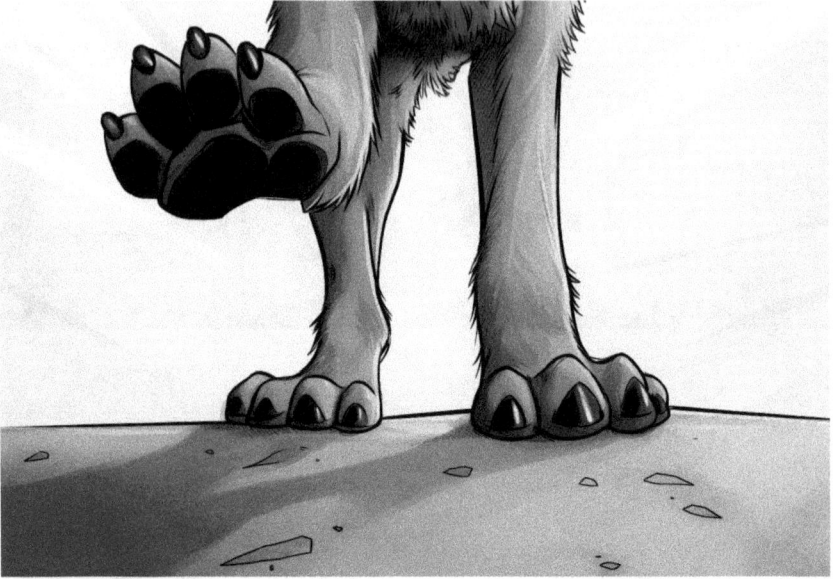

All dogs have an extra claw behind their front legs called a dewclaw. A lot of people assume that there's no modern purpose for these additional claws, but this is untrue. Dogs actually benefit greatly from having these claws; they are especially important when dogs are running at high speeds on slippery surfaces. Scientists have discovered that they provide extra traction and grip in order to ensure that dogs do not slip when running. They also help stabilize the carpal tunnel joint, also known as the rest joint, helping prevent a variety of injuries that may otherwise happen just by having slightly less support in that area. Some breeds even have these claws behind their back legs, where they serve a similar purpose. Some dog owners opt to dewclaw their pets, but veterinarians typically advise against this as it is considered an unnecessary procedure and is painful for the dog.

80. Why do woodpeckers peck wood?

Woodpeckers are known to peck at wood, whether it belongs to a tree, a post, or a building. This behavior can be quite vexing for homeowners and carpenters. However, it's essential to understand that woodpeckers are not intentionally trying to irritate humans; they are simply focused on their own survival and well-being. First and foremost, these birds primarily subsist on a diet of sap and insects. To access these vital food sources, they must excavate within trees. Consequently, they peck at the wood until they can reach the sap and insects. In addition, woodpeckers will also peck holes in dying trees in order to find a place to safely nest. Several other species of birds also benefit from this as nests that woodpeckers leave behind are often used by species of birds that cannot build their own nests. Finally, woodpeckers will attempt to make noise by pecking wood and other materials in order to draw attention from mates. This is why you will sometimes find the birds tapping their beaks on metal objects instead of wood.

Did You Know?

- Snails have thousands of tiny teeth located on their tongue-like radula.
- The tapeworm can grow up to 100 feet (thirty meters) long inside a host's intestines.
- Hummingbirds can consume up to half their body weight in nectar daily.
- Some species of geckos can walk on water due to specialized feet.
- The bombardier beetle produces a chemical reaction inside its abdomen to shoot hot, noxious chemicals at predators.
- The planarian flatworm is biologically immortal, as it can continuously regenerate itself.

81. Why do cats have whiskers?

No drawing of a cat is complete without adding whiskers. Why do cats have these weird hair-like structures to begin with? Cats have a variety of ways of assessing the world around them. They have a keen sense of sight, a good sense of hearing, and a pretty good sense of smell as well. Their sense of touch, however, is also extremely important. Whiskers help cats assess their environment through their sense of touch, primarily assisting them with navigation and balance. Studies have shown that the removal of a cat's whiskers will cause them to become disoriented and unbalanced. In addition, whiskers help cats determine the distance between them and other objects via vibrations in the air. This could be particularly helpful when chasing prey. Whiskers also help detect changes in the air that can indicate when a predator is approaching.

82. Why do some ants fly?

Have you ever seen an ant fly? Believe it or not, sometimes these creatures are not actually ants. Some species of termites resemble ants with wings. If one sees a flying ant, they should be certain to double check and make sure that it is not a termite. However, some species of ants do have members that fly. Flying ants do not generally bite humans and do not pose a threat to their homes like termite do. Some species of ants are called swarmers or alates; they swarm and travel in order to reproduce. There are three types of ants in the species: male, female, and worker. Worker ants are not able to fly at all, while both male and female ants will travel to reproduce. The bigger flying ants are often female, with the males being smaller. Seeing one or two of these flying ants generally is not an issue. However, if large amounts are seen, it can be a sign of an infestation.

83. Why do some ants smell like coconut?

Many people have experienced an interesting phenomenon when dealing with an ant infestation, where some ants seem to give off a coconutty scent. Only one species of ant is capable of giving off this odd odor. The odorous house ant is known to emit a rather peculiar smell, particularly when squished. The smell has been described as rotten coconuts, blue cheese, and penicillin-like. Some people find the smell to be closer to that of coconuts and almost smell rather pleasant; others find it to be disgusting and off putting. Why did these ants smell so hard? All ants use smells and pheromones to communicate with each other. Humans typically cannot smell these pheromones; unfortunately, we are capable of smelling the pheromones produced by this one species. The smells are not meant for us, but instead meant to communicate to the other ants that there is danger or food nearby.

84. Why do dogs chase the garbage truck?

Many owners have had to chase down their excited pups after the garbage truck made an unexpected visit down their street. Why are dogs so enamored with the idea of chasing the garbage truck? In general, some dogs are more prone to chasing vehicles than others. Dogs with a high prey drive may chase objects just because they are moving, even if the object is significantly larger than the dog itself. However, sometimes owners will find dogs that normally do not chase vehicles having a sudden interest in chasing the garbage truck. This is because of the variety of smells that come from the back of this vehicle. Dogs have a very strong sense of smell and are attracted to odors that we consider to be gross or hard to deal with. When the garbage truck passes, it releases the smell of garbage into the air which draws the interest of most dogs. Some dogs will want to follow the source of the smell in order to investigate.

85. Why do puffer fish puff up when scared?

Puffer fish are a unique type of fish with the ability to inflate when threatened. Some people find this ability to be frightening, while others find it to be entertaining and even keep the fish as pets. However, puffer fish inflate for a very important reason. Puffer fish are hunted by a variety of creatures, including large animals like dolphins. Before inflating, puffer fish are typically much smaller than their predators. Whenever they are pursued by a predator, they inflate and make it more difficult for the predator to eat them. If the predator has already managed to swallow them, this inflation can lead to the predator suffocating. Some puffer fish species also have spikes, which frequently contain toxins, providing additional protection against predators.

86. Why do goats fall over?

A few years ago, fainting goats became a social media hit, with thousands of videos popping up online of goats passing out when startled. While the idea of goats fainting due to fear can certainly be amusing, this is not what actually occurs when goats fall over after being startled. Goats remain fully conscious during this process. They are not fainting or passing out; instead, they are attempting to flee. Sometimes when they try to run away, they accidentally make the muscles go rigid in preparation to run. This can cause the muscles to temporarily lock up, resulting in the goats falling over and giving the appearance of fainting. The goats that do this are referred to as myotonic goats and they are born with a congenital disorder known as myotonia congenita (also known as Thomsen's Disease). While the condition is generally harmless to goats, it does cause them to inadvertently freeze up when startled.

87. Why do cats chase mice?

It has been documented throughout history that cats naturally love to chase and attack mice. Historians believe that this is one reason why cats have become domesticated over the years. Cats were drawn to human settlements because the large amount of grain that humans stored drew mice to the area. Over time, people realized the value of having cats around to kill mice as it reduced food waste and disease. Cats chase mice because they are natural carnivores. They do not eat plants so they are unable to forage for food. Instead, they must rely on their hunting skills to kill and eat prey. Due to their small size, cats are limited in what they are able to kill and eat. Birds and mice are often the easiest and most abundant prey that modern cats can find. While most pet cats are well fed and do not need to hunt, their instincts tell them to do so anyway. Therefore, most cats will chase mice if the opportunity presents itself.

88. Why do turtles have a shell?

Turtles are reptiles that have shells on the outside of their bodies. Technically, the shells are parts of their bodies and cannot be removed without harming the turtle. Most individuals assume that turtles have shells to protect them from predators. This is indeed one of the reasons why turtles have evolved to have shells over the years, but it's not the only one. In addition, some species of turtles have softer shells that provide little protection. Scientists have recently discovered that the original purpose of turtles having shells was not primarily for protection. It appears that turtles developed shells to grant themselves the ability to dig. Shells provided stability and leverage, enabling turtles to excavate the ground, thus facilitating their dual adaptation to life on both land and in water. Some scientists even believe that this adaptation may have been crucial in safeguarding them from extinction during significant extinction events.

89. Why do shrimp have that pointy part on their heads?

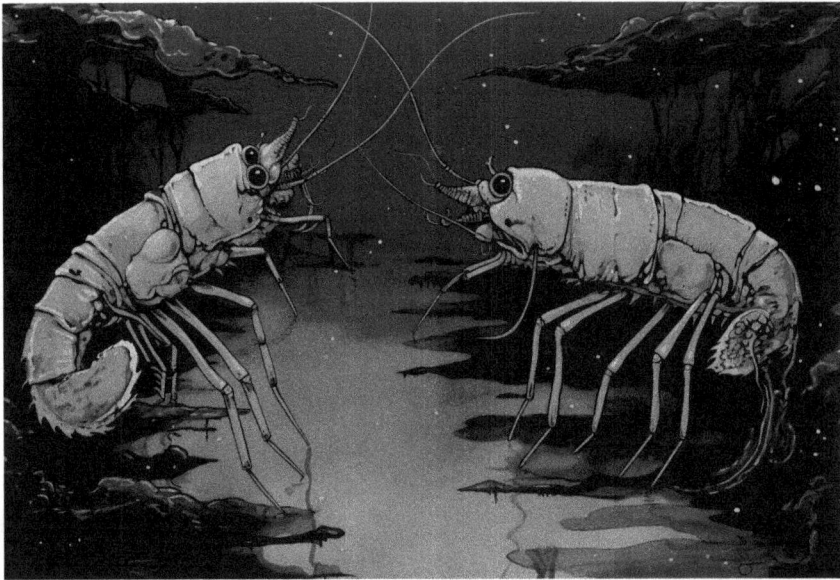

Have you ever been eating unpeeled shrimp and accidentally poked yourself with the pointy, horn-like structure on the top of the shrimp's head? This structure is called a rostrum, and despite how painful its poke can be, it's not meant to hurt humans. The rostrum has two primary purposes. First, it helps shrimp navigate their world and steer their bodies. Specifically, it helps them to maintain the proper angle and direction while swimming backward. However, this is not the only use for this body part. Shrimp will often fight each other and other sea creatures using the rostrum as a kind of sword. It can be used offensively, for attacking weaker shrimp or prey, as well as defensively, when shrimp are under attack by larger shrimp or predators. While this body part is not intended to harm humans, it can still deliver a painful poke and potentially lead to infection if left untreated.

90. Why do axolotls morph sometimes?

Axolotls are a type of salamander that are not supposed to grow past their tadpole stage. While most amphibians produce growth hormones until they become frogs or land-dwelling salamanders, the axolotl stops producing this hormone before it can begin to lose its gills. This creates a salamander that perpetually lives in water. However, sometimes axolotls will suddenly begin producing more growth hormone and will morph into a terrestrial or land dwelling salamander. This happens because another species of salamander, known as the tiger salamander, was interbred with axolotls when they began to gain popularity as pets. Tiger salamanders morph into terrestrial salamanders once they reach maturity. Some axolotls have genes left over from these tiger salamanders that cause them to suddenly begin to morph. It is believed that environmental factors play a role as well, with certain conditions, such as excessive heat, causing dormant genes to become active. However, there appears to be no way to predict which axolotls will morph and which won't.

Did You Know?

- The world's smallest mammal is the bumblebee bat, with a wingspan of only 5.7 inches (14.4 centimeters).
- The tiny poison dart frog's skin contains enough toxins to kill large predators.
- The pygmy goat is one of the smallest domesticated goats, standing about 16 inches (40.6 centimeters) tall.
- Shrews are small mammals with high metabolic rates, requiring them to eat their body weight daily.
- Dwarf hamsters, like the Roborovski, weigh just a few grams and are incredibly fast runners.
- The world's smallest chameleon, Brookesia micra, can fit on the tip of a matchstick.

91. Why do green anoles get darker?

Have you ever noticed that certain kinds of lizards, specifically green anoles, will sometimes go from light green to dark brown when upset? This is the green anole's way of expressing their displeasure with something happening in their immediate environment. One common reason these lizards may change color is their dissatisfaction with the temperature or lighting in their current location. This is more common in lizards that are kept as pets than those that are found in the wild. These lizards may also darken when attempting to resolve a territorial dispute with another lizard. They do this to intimidate the rival or to express their dissatisfaction at losing their territory. Female lizards may also turn brown when encountering male lizards they want to mate with, indicating that these lizards change color for reasons other than displeasure. Additionally, a lizard's health can influence its coloration. Dehydration, hormone issues, and illness can all lead to a lizard darkening in color.

92. Why do gorillas beat their chest?

Movies like *King Kong* have shown gorillas as large monkeys that spend a lot of time beating their chest. Is this an actual behavior that is common in gorillas or is it something that the movies have made up to make them seem more intimidating? While gorillas in the wild don't beat their chests nearly as often as those in movies, it is indeed a behavior that gorillas engage in. Female gorillas, in general, don't participate in this activity at all. Instead, it seems to be a behavior primarily displayed by male gorillas. Scientists suggest that this behavior likely serves as a display of dominance. The sound produced when gorillas beat their chests can demonstrate their size and strength. Male gorillas employ this technique to intimidate smaller, weaker males. Moreover, this action appears to attract female gorillas, as it showcases strength, which is impressive for the purpose of mating.

93. Why do vultures circle?

Have you ever noticed vultures circling a field while riding along the highway or playing outside? While many people think that vultures usually do this whenever they've found a meal, few know exactly why they specifically fly in circles. First of all, vultures don't typically circle around dead or dying animals. In fact, when vultures are seen circling, it signifies that they haven't found anything to eat yet and are potentially hoping to locate a meal. Sometimes they are circling above thermal air vents that release warm air from the Earth. This enables them to effortlessly glide and navigate through the air, making it easier for them to search for food. Often, you'll observe one bird flying lower than the rest, specifically scouting for potential meals on behalf of the group. Once a meal is located, the vultures in the group land to feed, without lingering in the air above the meal.

94. Why do some mosquitoes not bite?

Many people have noticed that some mosquitoes appear very eager to bite and feed on people's blood, while others seem less interested in this concept. There are a few reasons for this. First, only female mosquitoes actually bite and drink blood; male mosquitoes don't do this. Second, many species are often mislabeled as being mosquitoes. There are several types of flies that look very similar to mosquitoes but do not bite or suck blood. Often, when people claim that mosquitoes haven't bitten them, they have likely mistaken one of the fly species for mosquitoes. Third, certain individuals are less attractive to specific types of mosquitoes. Mosquitoes have varying preferences for their targets, influenced by factors such as body temperature, body odor, and the type of microbes present on a person's skin. While certain mosquitoes may be attracted to a person's odor or body temperature, these same factors may deter other mosquitoes from biting them.

95. Why do silverfish eat clothing?

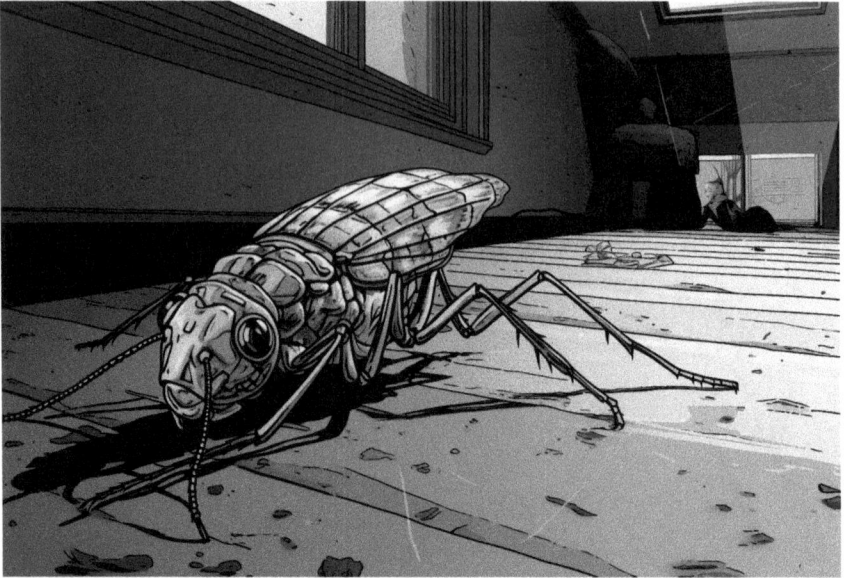

Silverfish are interesting-looking creatures that frequently roam bathrooms and closets. Many individuals are aware that they sometimes attempt to feed on clothing, leading to confusion regarding their particular interest in fabric. The truth is, silverfish do not want to eat your fabric; instead, they are more interested in some of the compounds found on your clothes. Silverfish have an appetite for starches, sugars, and proteins. Although they often search through kitchens before targeting clothing, this doesn't always deter them from exploring a closet and nibbling on clothes containing the mentioned substances. Clothing that has been starched is especially susceptible to silverfish consumption, as these insects have a general affinity for starch. Furthermore, clothing with stains from sugary beverages and food can also be attractive to silverfish. If you refrain from starching your clothes and generally keep them free of sugary stains, you shouldn't have to worry about silverfish considering them as a snack.

96. Why do bats sleep upside-down?

Movies often depict bats as creatures that sleep upside-down. This portrayal is mostly accurate. Among the hundreds of bat species, all but six sleep in an inverted position. The reason for this unique sleeping posture is related to their method of taking flight. Unlike birds, bats cannot lift themselves from the ground due to their wing structure. To initiate flight, they must begin by falling and then spread their wings. Consequently, they seek elevated roosting spots where they can hang upside-down, allowing them to simply release and commence their flight. This position also offers the advantage of easy takeoff in emergencies, while keeping them well-concealed from potential predators. Bats possess specialized tendons that automatically tighten, causing their talons to grip firmly while roosting, making upside-down sleep a natural and efficient choice for them.

97. Why do cats get scared when they see cucumbers?

Viral videos on the Internet have shown cats freaking out when exposed to cucumbers. Many people question if this is real and if so, why does it happen? Not all cats fear cucumbers; however, some do. These cats often jump in fright or puff up their fur to appear larger. This is because some cats mistake the cucumber for something else. While we cannot definitively determine what they perceive the cucumber as, scientists speculate that, at first glance, some cats may mistake it for a snake. While cats often play with snakes and even hunt them, snakes are also capable of harming cats. Therefore, when a cat encounters a cucumber unexpectedly, they may become scared or act defensively. Some cats may eventually calm down and investigate the cucumber further, while others often flee the scene. In the end, this reaction may seem irrational, but it is one of many instincts that help keep our beloved kitties safe from potential danger.

98. Why do lizards have a throat pouch?

Have you ever noticed that green anoles and some other types of lizards have red pouch-like organs on the bottom of their throat? While many people assume this is some sort of pouch, it is actually a flap of skin known as the dewlap or the throat fan. Special bones called the hyoid apparatus give these lizards the ability to display their dewlaps at will. Both male and female lizards possess special throat fans, but male lizards have a red throat fan, whereas female lizards typically have a whitish-gray throat fan. Female lizards only use their throat fans for displays involving mating, but male lizards have multiple uses for their dewlaps. Male lizards display their dewlaps to assert dominance over other male lizards. This is why you will sometimes see them displaying their dewlaps to each other while bobbing up and down. Both male and female lizards will also display their dewlaps in order to attract each other. You can tell exactly what encounter is going on by looking at the color of the dewlaps that each lizard involved has.

99. Why do cats spray?

Cats that have not been spayed or neutered sometimes engage in what we refer to as "spraying." In this behavior, cats release a stream of foul-smelling liquid from their rear end alongside a stream of urine. Cats often direct this stream at objects or walls. While this behavior can be frustrating for pet owners, it serves as an important communication component for cats. When cats spray objects, they are marking the object as their territory. This enables other cats to smell the object and understand that it has been claimed by another cat. Sometimes, this can lead to dominance battles, with two cats repeatedly spraying the same object in an attempt to assert ownership. Male cats are more likely to spray, but female cats will also spray on occasion. Some cats never spray, even if they remain unspayed or unneutered.

100. Why do dogs get scared during thunderstorms?

Most dogs are generally happy animals, but some can be easily frightened by loud noises or unexpected events. Many dogs have a fear of thunderstorms. While it's true that many dogs are afraid of the loud noise created by thunder, it's not the sole reason for their fear. Dogs can also sense changes in pressure that humans cannot perceive. Scientists have determined that these pressure changes can lead to anxiety in dogs, even in the absence of thunder. Additionally, the social aspects of storms can impact dogs, as they often find themselves alone during these events, with their owners at work or crating them due to anxiety, which can further increase their distress.

Did You Know?

- Mice are highly intelligent and can learn and solve complex puzzles.
- Elephant shrews have large ears, which they use to radiate excess heat and keep cool.
- A tiny creature called the water bear, or tardigrade, can survive extreme conditions, including space.
- Leafcutter ants are small but strong, capable of carrying leaves several times their body weight.
- The world's smallest deer, the pudu, stands just twelve-fourteen inches (thirty to thirty-five centimeters) tall at the shoulder.
- Sandpipers are small birds with long bills, ideal for probing the sand for tiny prey.
- Microscopic water fleas, or Daphnia, are essential in aquatic ecosystems, serving as a food source for many small animals.

101. Why do beavers build dams?

Beavers are renowned for their ability to break down large branches and logs with their front teeth to construct structures known as dams. However, many people are unaware of why beavers build dams. Beavers are, in essence, the architects and civil engineers of the animal world. They shape their environment to meet their needs, much like humans do. To ensure their safety, beavers require large bodies of water for swimming. While they may be slow and vulnerable on land, they are agile swimmers and can protect themselves in the water. When natural ponds are not available to them, beavers create their own by using branches, mud, and grass to obstruct riverways and streams, thus forming their own ponds. This behavior also assists them in accessing the vegetation and bark they need for sustenance. One common misconception is that beavers live inside their dams. In reality, they typically reside in special mounds located near their dams.

References

Bittel, Jason. "Five animals that can sense things you can't." Popular Science. https://www.popsci.com/alien-animal-senses/. Accessed September 27, 2023.

Bradbury, Jack W., and Vehrencamp, Sandra Lee. Principles of Animal Communication, Oxford University Press, 2011.

Dawkins, Marian Stamp. Observing Animal Behaviour: Design and Analysis of Quantitative Data, Oxford University Press, 2007.

Januaries, Frederick. "31 Dog Behaviors and What They Mean." PetHelpful. https://pethelpful.com/dogs/common-dog-behaviors-you-should-know-their-meaning. Accessed October 2, 2023.

Kappeler, Peter. Animal Behaviour, An Evolutionary Perspective, Springer, 2022.

Kaziukonis, Aivaras and Lyskoit, Violeta. "40 Weird Animal Behaviors That Are As Weird As They Are Impressive." Boredpanda. https://www.boredpanda.com/weird-animal-behaviors/. Accessed October 5, 2023.

Manning, Aubrey and Dawkins, Marian Stamp. An Introduction to Animal Behaviour, Cambridge University Press, 2012.

Rose, Elizabeth. Animal Adaptations for Survival, Rosen Publishing Group's PowerKids Press, 2005.

Rose, Wendy. "Decode Your Cat's Behavior: 17 Cat Behaviors Explained." Reader's Digest. https://www.rd.com/list/how-to-decode-your-cats-behavior/. Accessed September 25, 2023.

Shah, Sonia. "The Animals Are Talking. What Does It Mean?" The New York Times Magazine. https://www.nytimes.com/2023/09/20/magazine/animal-communication.html/. Accessed September 20, 2023.

Bonus!

Thanks for supporting me and purchasing this book! I'd like to send you some freebies. They include:

- The digital version of *500 World War I & II Facts*

- The digital version of *101 Idioms and Phrases*

- The audiobook for my best seller *1144 Random Facts*

Scan the QR code below, enter your email and I'll send you all the files. Happy reading!

Check out my other books!

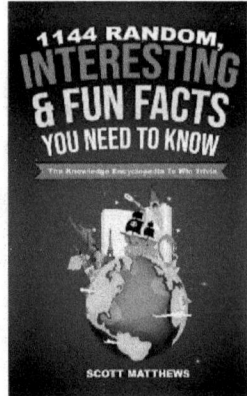

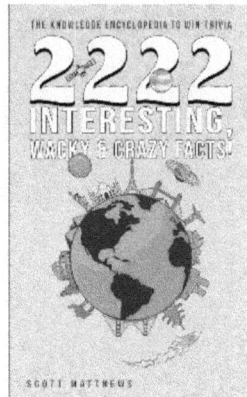

- 500 WORLD WAR I & II FACTS — Interesting Quizzes & History Information To Win Trivia — SCOTT MATTHEWS
- 1100 CRAZY FUN & RANDOM FACTS YOU WON'T BELIEVE — The Knowledge Encyclopedia To Win Trivia
- 1144 RANDOM, INTERESTING & FUN FACTS YOU NEED TO KNOW — The Knowledge Encyclopedia To Win Trivia — SCOTT MATTHEWS
- WHY DO WE SAY THAT? — 101 Idioms, Phrases, Sayings & Facts! A Brief History On Where They Come From! — SCOTT MATTHEWS
- Superstitions, Folklore, Myths & Legends — The Origins, History & Facts of Popular Known Tales — SCOTT MATTHEWS
- 2222 INTERESTING, WACKY & CRAZY FACTS! — THE KNOWLEDGE ENCYCLOPEDIA TO WIN TRIVIA — SCOTT MATTHEWS

www.ingramcontent.com/pod-product-compliance
Lightning Source LLC
Chambersburg PA
CBHW070124030426
42335CB00016B/2261